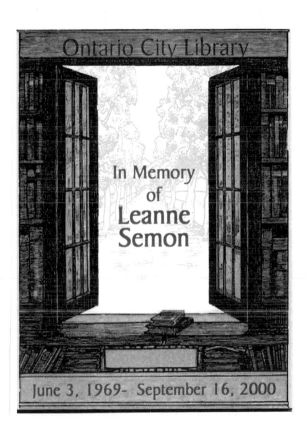

Ontario City Library

In Memory
of
**Leanne
Semon**

June 3, 1969- September 16, 2000

Look What Came From

England

by

Kevin Davis

Franklin Watts

A Division of Grolier Publishing

New York London Hong Kong Sydney

Danbury, Connecticut

Series Concept: Shari Joffe
Design: Steve Marton

Library of Congress Cataloging-in-Publication Data

Davis, Kevin A.
  Look What Came From England / by Kevin Davis.
    p. cm. — (Look what came from)
  Includes bibliographical references and index.
  Summary: Describes many things that originally came
from England, including inventions, sports and games,
food, vehicles, fashion, animals, and nursery rhymes.
    ISBN 0-531-11686-7 (lib.bdg.)   0-531-16434-9(pbk.)
  1. England—Civilization—Juvenile literature.
[1. England—Civilization. 2. Civilization, Modern—
English influences.] I. Title. II. Series: Look what
came from series.
DA115/D34 1999
942—dc21   99-19258
                                                    CIP
                                                    AC

Visit Franklin Watts on the Internet at:
http://publishing.grolier.com

Photo credits ©: Archive Photos: 21 left (Popperfoto), 27; Brian Seed: 19 top right;
Christie's Images: 6 right; Corbis-Bettmann: 9 (UPI), 3 bottom, 6 left, 10 left, 14,
15, 19 left; E.T. Archive: border on pages 4, 6-32, 7 (Victoria and Albert
Museum), 11 top right (British Museum), cover top right, 3 center, 10 bottom right,
11 left, 12, 18 left, 22 left, 23 top right; Envision: 17 top left (Dennis Galante), 16
top, 17 bottom left (Peter Johansky), 26 left (Overseas), 32 (Guy Powers), 16
bottom (Osentosky & Zoda); Galyn C. Hammond: 19 bottom right; National
Geographic Image Collection: 21 bottom right (George Mobley); Palma Allen: 23
bottom right; Photo Researchers: 11 bottom right (Pierre Berger), 10 top right (Dr.
Jeremy Burgess/SPL), cover left, 26 right (Aaron Haupt), 24 center
(Mero/Jacana), 17 bottom right (Robin Laurance), cover bottom right, 3 top, 24
left, 24 bottom (Renee Lynn), 13 left (Will & Deni McIntyre), 18 right (The Photo
Works); Stock Montage, Inc.: 8 right, 22 right, 22 center, 23 left; Superstock, Inc.:
25 (David David Gallery, Philadelphia), cover background, 8 left; Tony Stone
Images: 1, 6 center (Andy Roberts); TRIP: 17 top right (R. Bamber), 20 (J.
Ringland), 13 right (H. Rogers), 21 top right (M. Thornton); Viesti Collection, Inc.:
4 right (Photo Shot/BAVARIA).
Map by Charise Mericle.

Contents

Greetings from England!

The flag of
Great Britain

You might be surprised at all the things you see every day that come from England. The sandwich you eat for lunch, the mattress on your bed, and the television set you watch are just some of the things invented in this amazing country.

England is a fascinating place. It is the largest country in a nation called Great Britain, which includes Scotland, Wales, and Northern Ireland. All of these countries are part of Northern Europe.

More than 1,500 years ago, England was part of the Roman Empire. Since then, many different people from Europe have brought their own traditions, customs, and languages to England. The main language that developed is the one you're reading: English!

Let's take a trip and find out what comes from this great country!

Inventions

Many children save pennies in a **piggy bank.** Did you know that the piggy bank came from England in the 1700s? It wasn't really called a piggy bank at first. English people used to make jars from a type of clay called pygs, which sounds just like "pigs." Sometimes people stored money in the jars. Later, someone came up with the idea of making a little pig-shaped bank from this type of clay.

Lots of interesting inventions, many of which you may use, came from England. Have you ever looked through a **magnifying glass?** This great invention that makes things look bigger was made by an English man named Robert Grosseteste about 800 years ago. Because of his discovery, other scientists were able to build telescopes to see planets and stars.

Piggy bank

Everyone knows you can't send a letter without a stamp. The first **postage stamp** was made in England more than 150 years ago.

Magnifying glass

An English stamp from the 1850s (top) and a current English stamp (bottom)

One of the first Christmas cards

After postage stamps were invented, an English man got an idea for a fun thing to send through the mail. In 1843, Henry Cole asked a friend to draw a card that showed a family celebrating Christmas. It was the first **Christmas card.** Today, people all over the world send Christmas cards.

more inventions

Modern-day stapler

Do you ever staple papers together in school?

The first **stapler** was invented in England in 1868. It wasn't used for paper, though. It was used to fasten together pieces of leather to make shoes!

One of the most popular inventions from England is the **television.** There were many inventors who tried to make the first television. But a scientist named

John Logie Baird was the first man to transmit a TV picture in 1926. The very first television picture was the head of a doll named Bill. A boy who worked with Baird got to be the first real person to have his picture on TV!

The first television machine

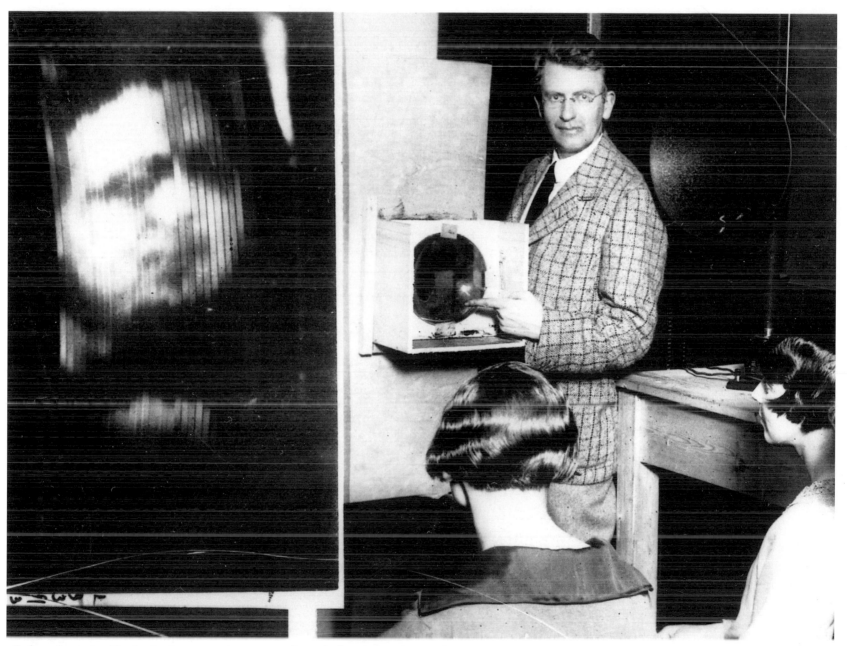

John Logie Baird demonstrating his television machine

Transportation

When you were very little, you probably were wheeled around in a **baby carriage.** The first baby carriage was invented in England in 1733. It was designed by a man named William Kent for the children of an English duke. The first carriage was shaped like a seashell and looked a little bit like a shoe. It was made to be pulled by a dog or small pony!

Have you ever been on a **train?** This very important invention came from England in 1803. An engineer named Richard Trevithick built the first steam locomotive to travel on railroad tracks. He gave it a funny name: "Catch-me-who-can." The first train didn't go very far. It went around in a circle to show people how it worked.

Train on the Liverpool and Manchester Railway in 1831

10   Baby carriage from the late 1800s

After the locomotive was invented, people in England built the very first **railroad** to take people from one place to another. In 1830, the first railroad line was opened between the English cities of Liverpool and Manchester.

Around the same time that the train was invented, the first **motorized bus** was built in England. It had 6 wheels, 18 seats, and was powered by a steam engine. The man who invented the bus, Sir Goldsworthy Gurney, drove it from London to a town called Bath. People loved the bus so much that a short time later, regular bus service began. Today, England is very famous for its bright red **double-decker buses.**

The first motorized bus

Double-decker bus

Around the Kitchen

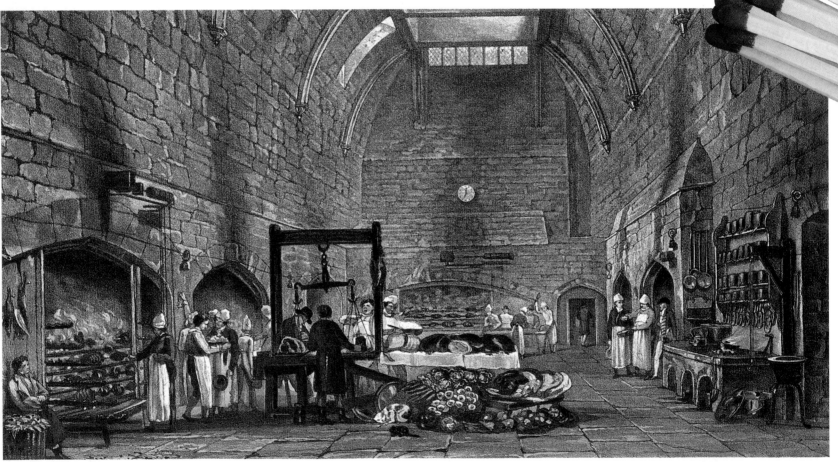

This 19th-century drawing of a kitchen of British royalty shows a kitchen range on the far right.

12

For thousands of years, people all over the world cooked their food on an open fire. The first **kitchen range** was invented in England more than 300 years ago to make cooking easier. It allowed people to put their pots and pans on a flat surface. Early kitchen ranges were made of bricks heated by a fire burning underneath. Later, metal ranges were invented.

Long ago, people used to make fire by rubbing sticks together, which created sparks because of friction. But did you know that the first **matches** were made in England? A scientist named John Walker discovered how to make matches by accident in 1826. He was mixing some chemicals with a stick when a small teardrop formed at the end. He tried to scrape it off on the floor, and it caught fire!

Have you ever used a **Thermos** to hold your drinks? This amazing container keeps liquids either hot or cold. It was invented in 1892 by a scientist named Sir James Dewar. The container was first used to store medicines and even tropical fish! When people found out how well it kept drinks hot or cold, they began using it on camping trips and picnics.

Modern-day thermos

Around the House

The first lawn mower

Many things that make life easier around the house were invented in England. Cutting grass used to be a very difficult chore. People used long blades called scythes to trim the grass by hand. An English gardener named Edwin Budding made it easier when he built the first hand-operated **lawn mower** in 1830. Budding's machine had sharp rotating blades. He thought that using it would be a fun way for people to get exercise.

If you've ever jumped on your bed, you can thank the English for inventing the **spring mattress.** For thousands of years, people slept on beds of straw, pine needles, or leaves. No one knows exactly who invented the spring mattress, but and carpets and sucking in the dirt and dust! He choked from the dust, but began using cloths over his mouth to trap it. The first vacuum cleaner was built in 1901 and was the size of a refrigerator. Two people were needed to move it from house to house. Eventually, smaller vacuum cleaners were made.

Early spring mattresses

springs began being used in chairs and couches in England hundreds of years ago. In the 1870s, people began sleeping on top of blanket-covered springs and found it very comfortable. Soon springs were put inside mattresses.

One of the most useful household appliances is the **vacuum cleaner.** Its inventor, H. Cecil Booth, conducted his research by putting his mouth on furniture

The first vacuum cleaner

Food

Modern-day sandwich

What's your favorite kind of sandwich? Peanut butter and jelly? Ham and cheese? Bologna? Whatever you like to put between two pieces of bread, you can thank a hungry English man for inventing the **sandwich.** It's actually named after the town where this man lived. John Montagu, known as the Earl of Sandwich, liked to play cards. One day in 1762, he didn't want to leave the table where he was playing, so he ordered slices of meat and cheese stuffed between two pieces of bread. This allowed him to hold his food in one hand and play cards with the other!

What would a sandwich be without cheese? **Cheddar cheese,** one of the most popular cheeses in the world, originally came from England. It was named after the town of Cheddar, where it was first made more than 400 years ago.

Salisbury steak was named after Dr. James Henry Salisbury, who told people in the 1800s that it was good to shred their food to make it easier to digest. His Salisbury steak was similar to the

Cheddar cheese

16

Salisbury steak

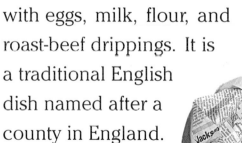

Shepherd's pie

Fish and chips

popular "Hamburg steak," or hamburger, from Germany, but it was oval-shaped and served on a plate with gravy instead of on a bun.

One of the most popular foods in England is **Yorkshire pudding,** a puffy, breadlike side dish made

Small Yorkshire puddings

with eggs, milk, flour, and roast-beef drippings. It is a traditional English dish named after a county in England.

The English also enjoy **shepherd's pie,** a casserole of ground meat and mashed potatoes. **Fish and chips** are also very popular and are sold at shops.

Fashion

top hat

English men wearing derbies

Have you ever seen a magician pull a rabbit out of a hat? That tall black hat, called a **top hat,** was first made in England in 1730. Men originally wore top hats while they were fox hunting. They made their hats big and tall so that their heads would be protected if they fell off their horses!

Another hat, the **derby,** was invented in England in the 1780s. This hat was shaped like a melon and was also called a "bowler." Englishmen wore these hats to the horse races.

To prevent their pants from falling down, Englishmen started wearing **suspenders** in the 1700s. They were first called "gallowses" or "braces." They were made of cloth, went over the shoulders, and were buttoned to pants.

A jacket called the **blazer** was designed in England in the late 1800s. Most of the time, men wore these jackets at sporting events such as cricket matches, tennis matches, or boat races. Men on boating teams wore them because they wanted to look better than their competitors. Their blazers displayed the names of their schools or teams.

English schoolboys wearing blazers

Modern-day button-down shirt

The **button-down collar** was invented in England in the 1890s. It was designed to keep the shirt collars of polo players from flapping in the wind.

1870s advertisement for suspenders

Sports and Entertainment

Modern-day English circus bus

Children everywhere love to go to the circus. The first **traveling circus** originated in England in 1768 when a man named Philip Astley put on a big show with animals that performed amazing stunts and tricks. His show was so popular that Astley took it to other towns. Soon clowns, jugglers, and acrobats became part of the show.

A very popular sport in England is **rugby,** which was invented in the 1800s. Players kick and carry an oval-shaped ball across a big grass field toward a goal. There are 15 members on each team, and they are allowed to tackle each other.

England's national sport is **cricket.** The game dates back to the 1500s, and is played with two teams using a bat and ball. The bats look like big paddles.

Lawn bowling is also a popular sport in England. It is not like bowling at a bowling alley. Players roll balls on a grass lawn and try to get it closer to other balls to score points. England has many lawn-bowling clubs.

Cricket

Rugby

Lawn bowling

"Humpty Dumpty"

Stories and

"Jack and Jill"

"Three Blind Mice"

Have you heard the story of **"Humpty Dumpty,"** who sat on a wall and had a great fall? What about the song **"Three Blind Mice"?** About 500 years ago, parents of English children began telling stories and singing songs that many of us know today.

Nursery Rhymes

Other famous songs and nursery rhymes that came from England are **"Jack and Jill," "Old Mother Hubbard,"** and **"Little Miss Muffet."**

One of the most popular stories that came from England is **"Goldilocks and the Three Bears."** Did you know that when the story was first told in the 1800s, Goldilocks was an old woman? The story was later changed because people thought children would like it better if Goldilocks were a little girl.

"Little Miss Muffet"

Old Mother Hubbard
Went to the cupboard
To get her poor dog a bone;
But when she came there
The cupboard was bare,
And so the poor dog had none.

"Old Mother Hubbard"

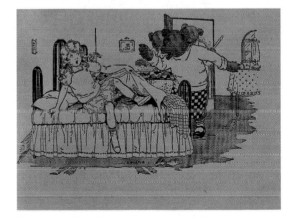

"Goldilocks and the Three Bears"

Pets

Cocker spaniel

Beagle

English people love their pets, especially their dogs. Many famous dog breeds came from England. Some of these dogs were first used to help people hunt.

One of the friendliest and most popular dogs that came from England is the **beagle.** This breed has been around for more than a thousand years!

Other dogs that came from England include the **cocker spaniel,** the **bulldog,** and the **English setter.**

Bulldog

English setters

Making Sandwiches

Sandwiches have come a long way since the Earl of Sandwich had the first one in 1762. Today, people make them out of all kinds of ingredients!

You can invent any kind of sandwich you like by putting your favorite fillings between two pieces of any kind of bread.

Some people like to put sliced bananas instead of jelly on their peanut butter sandwiches. Other people like to make sandwiches with lots of vegetables. Use your imagination. Here are a few suggestions to get started:

You'll need:

- Any kind of sliced bread or rolls
- Fillings, such as:
  - Sliced meats: ham, turkey, bologna, salami, or roast beef
  - Sliced cheese
  - Lettuce, tomatoes, onions, or other vegetables
  - Peanut butter and jelly
- Mustard, mayonnaise, ketchup, relish, or other favorite spreads
- A spoon and a knife

Once you have all of your ingredients, it's really easy to make a sandwich. Start by using a spoon or butter knife to spread the mustard or mayonnaise on one side of bread. Then put on some meat, lettuce, and tomato, and put the other piece of bread on top. Ask an adult to slice the sandwich for you. Some people like to slice off the crust of the bread and cut the sandwiches into little triangles.

This is very popular in England. If you make these little sandwiches, you can share them with your friends and try some of the sandwiches they have created!

How do you say....?

Although people from the United States and England speak the same language, they use different words to describe certain everyday things. Here are some examples.

England	United States
biro	ballpoint pen
bonnet	car hood
boot	car trunk
call box	phone booth
jumper	sweater
lift	elevator
nappy	baby diaper
petrol	gasoline
torch	flashlight
plimsoles	tennis shoes
sweet	candy
wireless	radio

To find out more

Here are some other resources to help you learn more about England:

Books

Blashfield, Jean F. **England** (Enchantment of the World series). Children's Press, 1997.

Burgan, Michael. **England** (True Book series). Children's Press, 1999.

Lace, William W. **England** (Modern Nations of the World). Lucent Books, 1997.

Lychak, William. **England** (Games People Play). Children's Press, 1995

Peplow, Mary. **England.** Steck-Vaughn Library, 1990.

Organizations and Online Sites

British Tourist Authority
http://www.visitbritain.com
Pictures, facts, figures, and travel information about England, Scotland, Wales, and Northern Ireland.

Destination England
http://www.lonelyplanet.com.au/ dest/eur/eng.htm
A travel guide from Lonely Planet with a slide show, maps, history, and major attractions in England.

England City Net
http://www.citynet/countries/ united_kingdon/england
Find out about weather, sports, and news from England. Also includes many links to interesting information about the country.

Global Friends: Discover England!
http://www.globalfriends.com/ html/world_tour/england/ england.htm
Answers interesting questions about England in the areas of language and expressions, daily life, celebrations, and creative arts.

United Kingdom
http://www.odci.gov/cia/ publications/factbook/uk.html
Lots of information on England's geography, people, government, economy, communications, and transportation.

Glossary

acrobat a person who is skilled in tumbling or gymnastics

casserole a food cooked or baked in a covered dish

describe to tell what something is about

develop to make

discover to find something new

Europe a continent located between Asia and the Atlantic Ocean

fashion a style that is popular

fasten to put together

friction rubbing one object against another

gamble to play a game for money or a prize

laboratory a place where scientists work and conduct experiments

lenses pieces of glass that make things look bigger or help a person see more clearly

modern occurring in the present time

originated began

polo a game in which players on horseback use mallets to drive a wooden ball into the opponent's goal

rotate to turn around

scientist a person who studies nature, biology, chemistry, or physics, and conducts experiments

similar like something else, but not exactly the same

traditions customs or ways of life handed down from generation to generation

transmit to send; move from one place to another

Index

Look what doesn't come from England!

The **English muffin** didn't really come from England. It is from the United States. In the late 1800s, an English man named Samuel Thomas moved to New York and began baking muffins similar to those he had eaten in England. He called them "English muffins" even though in England these were just called "muffins."

Meet the Author

Kevin Davis loves to travel and write about the interesting places he has visited. He lives in Chicago and is an author and journalist. This book is dedicated to Rowena Burkinshaw, a world traveler and adventurer who gave Kevin the travel bug.